W9-CFB-810

DOG HEROES ®

BRAVE HEARTS

by Meish Goldish

Consultant: Laurie Bergman, VMD
Diplomate American College of Veterinary Behaviorists
Keystone Veterinary Behavior Services
Villanova, PA

BEARPORT PUBLISHING

New York, New York

Credits

Cover and Title Page, © Vkarlov/Shutterstock; TOC, © Dominic Lipinski/PA Wire/Associated Press; 4, © PHB.cz (Richard Semik)/Shutterstock; 5, © Michele Leatherbury, DVM/Atlantic Animal Hospital; 6, © Michele Leatherbury, DVM/Atlantic Animal Hospital; 7, © Michele Leatherbury, DVM/Atlantic Animal Hospital; 8, © Nata Sdobnikova/Shutterstock; 9, © Sonya Etchison/Shutterstock; 10L, © Universal News & Sport (Scotland); 10, © Dan Flake/Shutterstock; 11, © Jan Daly/Shutterstock; 12, © 2010 Brian Smale; 13L, © 2010 Brian Smale; 13R, © Universal News & Sport (Scotland); 14, © FOX59 News; 15, © FOX59 News; 16TL, © TK; 16TR, © LivingPrimeTime.com; 16, © Malivan Iuliia/Shutterstock; 17, © Niagara Region Park Interpretive Programs Office; 18, © Michael Dalder/Reuters; 19, © craigrobinsonphoto/Thinkstock; 20, © The People's Dispensary for Sick Animals; 21, © bigfatgoth/Wikipedia; 22, © Juniors Bildarchiv GmbH/Alamy; 23, © John Alevroyiannis image provided by Canine Partners; 24, © The People's Dispensary for Sick Animals; 25, © Dominic Lipinski/PA Wire/Associated Press; 25B, © The People's Dispensary for Sick Animals; 26, © Tina Fineberg/Associated Press; 27, © Tina Fineberg/Associated Press; 28, © Todd Smarr/Courtesy of Denver Post; 29TL, © Susan Schmitz/Shutterstock; 29TR, © Kalmatsuy/Shutterstock; 29BL, © Eric Isselee/Shutterstock; 29BR, © Eric Isselee/Shutterstock.

Publisher: Kenn Goin
Senior Editor: Joyce Tavolacci
Creative Director: Spencer Brinker
Design: Dawn Beard Creative
Photo Researcher: We Research Pictures, LLC

Library of Congress Cataloging-in-Publication Data

Goldish, Meish, author.
  Brave hearts / by Meish Goldish.
    pages cm. — (Dog heroes)
  Includes bibliographical references and index.
  ISBN 978-1-62724-516-6 (library binding) — ISBN 1-62724-516-2 (library binding)
  1. Dogs—Anecdotes—Juvenile literature. 2. Animal heroes—Anecdotes—Juvenile literature. I. Title.
  II. Series: Dog heroes.
  SF426.5.G644 2015
  636.7088'7—dc23
                              2014035730

For more information, write to Bearport Publishing Company, Inc., 45 West 21st Street, Suite 3B, New York, New York 10010. Printed in the United States of America.

10 9 8 7 6 5 4 3 2 1

Table of Contents

Taking a Bullet

Late one night in July 2013, a man was standing outside his Virginia home when four armed robbers suddenly approached him. They forced the man into the house, where his wife and children were asleep. Then they began to steal items from the home. Lefty, the family's pit bull, sensed something was wrong and kept a close eye on the **intruders**.

The robbers planned their attack at night so it would be harder for them to be spotted.

Suddenly, one of the men pointed a gun at the father. Lefty sprang into action, fearlessly leaping in front of the **weapon** to protect her owner. The gunman fired, and the bullet struck the dog. The robbers then fled the house. Lefty was badly injured but alive. The brave-hearted **canine** had saved her owner's life!

The bullet **shattered** Lefty's right shoulder and damaged her right front leg.

Lefty, the family's pet pit bull

Losing and Winning

After being shot, Lefty was rushed to nearby Atlantic Animal Hospital. Doctors were unable to save the dog's damaged right front leg and had to **amputate** it. Luckily, however, the tough canine quickly recovered. She soon learned to walk and run on only three legs.

Lefty recovering after surgery

Because of all the **medical** treatment she received, Lefty had a big hospital bill that her family could not afford to pay. Workers at the animal hospital put Lefty's amazing story on the hospital's Facebook page. Many readers were so impressed by the dog's bravery that they sent **donations** to help out. These gifts ended up covering nearly all of Lefty's medical costs!

Dr. Michele Leatherbury, owner of Atlantic Animal Hospital in Accomac, Virginia, with Lefty

Atlantic Animal Hospital's Facebook page about Lefty received nearly 5,000 views.

Brave for a Reason

Many pet dogs, like Lefty, are very **loyal** to their owners and will act bravely to protect them—but why? Some people think it's because the dogs depend on their owners for food and shelter. However, **veterinary behaviorist** Dr. Laurie Bergman has a deeper explanation for this behavior.

Dogs are known for their loyalty to humans. That's why they are often called "man's best friend."

"Dogs are social animals. Just like people, they live in tight-knit groups," Dr. Bergman explains. "Over tens of thousands of years of **domestication**, dogs have become excellent at understanding human emotions. They are able to tell when people are afraid or hurt. So they react when a human family member is threatened or scared as they would if the human were a member of their canine family." In some cases, dogs will even risk their lives to protect those they care about.

Many dogs and their human family members have a very close bond.

Experts believe that dogs come from wolves and were domesticated around 130,000 years ago.

A Deadly Attack

To protect their owners, some brave dogs have dared to fight off much larger, fiercer animals. One evening in January 2010, an 11-year-old boy named Austin Forman went outside to collect firewood in the backyard of his home in Canada. As Austin got closer to the woodshed, he saw a large, scary animal with round ears and sharp teeth. Luckily, Austin had brought Angel, his golden retriever, with him.

Austin Forman

Suddenly, the large animal—a fierce cougar—leaped at Austin. Angel bravely jumped in front of the cougar to save the boy. Austin then raced into his house to get help as Angel and the cougar fought. The cougar **viciously** attacked the golden retriever, **clamping** its jaws around the dog's head.

A golden retriever weighs about 65 pounds (29.5 kg). That's less than half the weight of an adult cougar.

A cougar, also known as a mountain lion, is a large cat that is strong enough to kill a moose.

Going Head to Head

Austin raced inside his house, screaming, "There's a cougar eating Angel!" His terrified mother called the police. When an officer arrived, Angel's head was still trapped in the cougar's jaws. The officer took aim at the cougar and fired his gun. He hit the back end of the cat.

Austin and his mother with Chad Gravelle, the officer who shot the cougar, outside the Formans' home

When the cougar kept up its attack, the officer was forced to fire again. This time, he killed the animal. Luckily, Angel wasn't shot. However, she was badly hurt from the fight. Austin's parents rushed Angel to a **veterinarian** who treated her injuries. The Forman family was incredibly grateful that both Austin and Angel were safe. They were especially thankful to Angel for saving Austin's life. The brave-hearted canine had lived up to her name!

Angel was badly hurt but survived the cougar attack.

After Angel got away from the cougar, the injured dog walked over to Austin and sniffed him as if to make sure the boy was all right.

Angel wore a special collar to protect her head while her injuries healed.

13

Fire!

Nick Lamb of Indianapolis, Indiana, always knew that his dog, Ace, was a good friend. However, the 13-year-old boy never knew how brave the pit bull was until one afternoon in July 2014. Nick, who is **deaf**, was home taking a nap when a fire broke out in the garage. Because Nick wasn't wearing his hearing aids at the time, he didn't know the smoke alarms were beeping as smoke started to enter the house.

The fire spread from the garage to the house, where Nick was napping.

When Ace smelled the smoke, he began to lick Nick's face to wake him up. Nick, half-asleep, thought the dog wanted to be fed or walked and ignored him. Ace kept licking the boy until he finally woke up. Then Nick saw the smoke and raced out of the house with Ace to safety. Later, Nick said of his dog hero, "He saved my life. I love him a lot."

Nick (right) and his lifesaving hero, Ace

Ace woke Nick up just in time. After the pair escaped the house, the entire building burned down.

A Snowy Trap

Brave dogs can do more than alert their owners to danger. They can also help carry their owners to safety. On the evening of October 12, 2006, Eve and Norman Fertig, an elderly couple, were feeding animals at their **wildlife sanctuary** in Alden, New York. Suddenly, they got caught in a terrible snowstorm that knocked down trees and power lines all around them. The fallen trees blocked the Fertigs' only path back to their house, leaving them trapped outside in the freezing weather.

Eve and Norman Fertig

Powerful October storms in New York can bring wind and heavy snow that can knock down trees and power lines.

16

Luckily, the Fertigs' huge dog, Shana, was nearby. The German shepherd-wolf mix saw that her owners were in trouble. She began to dig an escape path underneath the fallen trees, using her claws and teeth. As Shana tore into the snowy ground, the Fertigs grew colder and more afraid. Eve told her husband, "I think we could die out here." Could Shana save them?

The Enchanted Forest Wildlife Sanctuary has several buildings in the woods, including the Fertigs' home.

The Enchanted Forest Wildlife Sanctuary, owned by Eve Fertig, provides care and shelter for injured and **orphaned** animals, such as birds and rabbits.

Pulling Through

After two hours, Shana finished digging a tunnel through the snow. It stretched all the way from the spot where the Fertigs were trapped to their house. Grabbing the sleeve of Eve's jacket, Shana yanked and pulled the tiny woman onto her back. Norman grabbed Eve's legs. Then the powerful canine began to haul her owners through the tunnel under the fallen trees!

Large German shepherds like Shana have powerful leg muscles that they can use to dig through snow.

Several hours later, in the middle of the night, Shana and the Fertigs finally reached their house. "It was the most heroic thing I've ever seen in my life," Eve said.

The house had no heat or electricity, due to the downed power lines. Cold and weak, the couple fell inside on the floor. They lay there until morning, with Shana lying close to them to keep them warm. "She kept us alive. She really did," Eve said.

Shana received the Citizens for Humane Animal Treatment Hero Award for her lifesaving actions.

After Shana's story made national news, people across the country sent toys to the dog and donated money to the Fertigs' wildlife sanctuary.

Downhill Disaster

Orca is another dog that would stop at nothing to help his human companion. One afternoon in May 2003, Cheryl Smith, a college student, was riding in her electric wheelchair along a dirt path in Heslington, England. Running at Cheryl's side was her **service dog**, Orca. Suddenly, the wheelchair struck a rock, sending Cheryl tumbling down a 15-foot (4.6 m) **embankment** into a ditch filled with water.

Cheryl and her service dog, Orca

pdsa
for pets in need of vets

Cheryl Smith

CAN
PARTNER

Cheryl was unable to move, trapped under her heavy 297-pound (135 kg) chair. Her loyal dog Orca wanted to stay with her, but Cheryl **commanded** the golden retriever to get help. He ran to find someone. However, the person Orca found thought the dog was lost and started to walk him home. What would Orca do now to try to save Cheryl?

As a service dog, Orca has been trained to get help if his owner is in trouble.

Orca had been Cheryl's service dog for only five weeks when the wheelchair accident happened.

21

A Daring Rescue

Orca struggled to get away from the person walking him. The determined dog broke free of his collar and raced back to Cheryl. Once again she commanded the canine to get help. Orca obeyed and ran off to find help a second time.

Orca ran as fast as he could to find help for Cheryl.

After running for a mile (1.6 km), Orca found a jogger named Peter Harrison, who happened to be Cheryl's neighbor. Peter could tell that Orca wanted to lead him somewhere, so he followed the dog. Orca led Peter to Cheryl, and Peter then phoned for help. Luckily, Cheryl was not seriously hurt. She praised Orca, saying, "He really came through for me."

Orca helps Cheryl care for her young daughter, Lily.

Three years after her wheelchair accident, Cheryl got married. Three tiny figures appeared on her wedding cake—the bride, the groom, and her brave dog, Orca!

It's an Honor

For his brave actions, Orca got more than just praise from Cheryl. The golden retriever also received a special award—the PDSA Gold Medal. It is the highest honor given to non-**military** animals for bravery in the United Kingdom.

Cheryl's dog Orca received the PDSA Gold Medal in 2006.

More than 20 canines have been awarded the PDSA Gold Medal. Some are police dogs that helped capture dangerous criminals. Other medal winners are **search-and-rescue dogs** that helped find victims of the 2005 London **terrorist** attacks. Many of the dogs, like Orca, helped save people in serious trouble.

This brave police dog and PDSA medal winner, Anya, saved her handler from a knife attack.

PDSA stands for the "People's Dispensary for Sick Animals." It is an organization in the United Kingdom that provides free veterinary care to sick and injured animals that belong to people in need.

The PDSA Gold Medal

pdsa
FOR ANIMAL GALLANTRY OR DEVOTION TO DUTY

Canine Lifesaver

Some brave dogs don't just win awards. They also become TV stars. One day in March 2007, Debbie Parkhurst of Calvert, Maryland, was eating an apple when a piece of it got stuck in her throat. She began to choke and had trouble breathing. Toby, her golden retriever, watched as Debbie tried to perform the **Heimlich maneuver** on herself to **dislodge** the fruit. When that failed, Debbie began pounding on her chest with her fists.

Debbie
Parkhurst
and Toby

Suddenly, Toby stood on his back legs and pushed Debbie to the floor. "He began jumping up and down on my chest," remembers Debbie. Then the apple piece popped out! Debbie was amazed. After Toby's incredible **feat** made national news, the golden retriever was invited to appear as a guest on a late night TV talk show. Toby's TV fame proves that everyone—not just grateful dog owners—loves brave dogs!

Debbie with Toby, who is about to receive a special award for his bravery

For his bravery, Toby received the 2007 Dog of the Year award from the American Society for the Prevention of Cruelty to Animals (ASPCA).

Just the Facts

- In 2010, Kenai, a Bernese mountain dog mix, was named Valor Dog of the Year by the Humane Society of the United States. The dog saved nine people at a vacation house in Colorado after she smelled gas leaking from a stove. Her repeated barking awoke her owner, who was able to lead everyone to safety.

- The American Humane Association presents the Stillman Award to animals or people who risk their lives to save others. One winner was a Rottweiler named Eve, who rescued her owner, Kathie Vaughn, from a burning truck.

- Rocky, a Labrador retriever, received a medal of bravery from the Royal Canadian Humane Association after saving a young girl from drowning. Rocky's owner saw two young girls who had fallen into an icy river. He pulled one girl ashore but couldn't reach the other one. Rocky swam out and rescued the second girl, saving her life.

Kenai, the Bernese mountain dog mix

Common Breeds: BRAVE DOGS

Any kind of dog can show bravery.
Here are several dog breeds featured in this book.

Pit bull

Golden retriever

German shepherd

Labrador retriever

amputate (AM-pyuh-tayt) to cut off a body part, such as an arm or leg

canine (KAY-nine) a member of the dog family

clamping (KLAMP-ing) holding in place tightly

commanded (kuh-MAND-id) gave an order

deaf (DEF) not able to hear

dislodge (diss-LOJ) to force something out of position

domestication (duh-MESS-tuh-*kay*-shuhn) when animals are tamed so they can live with people

donations (doh-NAY-shuhnz) items or money given as gifts

embankment (em-BANGK-muhnt) a high wall of land that is built to hold back water

feat (FEET) an achievement that shows great courage, strength, or skill

Heimlich maneuver (HIME-lik muh-NOO-vur) an emergency action done to remove food stuck in a person's throat, performed by squeezing the person from behind, below the ribs

intruders (in-TROOD-urs) people who go somewhere without permission

loyal (LOI-uhl) faithful to others

medical (MED-uh-kuhl) having to do with doctors or medicine

military (MIL-uh-*ter*-ee) having to do with the armed forces of a country, such as the army

orphaned (OR-fuhnd) having no parents

search-and-rescue dogs (SURCH-AND-RES-kyoo DAWGZ) dogs that look for lost people or survivors after a disaster such as an earthquake

service dog (SUR-viss DAWG) a dog that is trained to help a person who is disabled in some way

shattered (SHAT-urd) broke into tiny pieces

terrorist (TER-ur-ist) having to do with individuals or groups that use violence to get what they want

veterinarian (*vet*-ur-uh-NER-ee-uhn) a doctor who takes care of animals

veterinary behaviorist (VET-ur-uh-*ner*-ee bi-HAYV-yor-ist) an expert who understands the reasons why animals act in certain ways

viciously (VISH-uhss-lee) done in a dangerous way

weapon (WEP-uhn) something such as a gun or knife that can be used in a fight to defend or attack

wildlife sanctuary (WILDE-life SANGK-choo-er-ee) an area in nature where wild animals are protected

Bibliography

Bacon, Lance M. *Hero Dogs: Secret Missions and Selfless Service.* New York: White Star (2012).

Collins, Ace. *Man's Best Hero: True Stories of Great American Dogs.* Nashville, TN: Abingdon Press (2014).

Jackson, Donna M. *Hero Dogs: Courageous Canines in Action.* New York: Little Brown (2003).

Jones, Peter C., and Lisa MacDonald. *Hero Dogs: 100 True Stories of Daring Deeds.* Kansas City, MO: Andrews McMeel (2012).

Read More

Camerena, Rebecca. *My Dog Is a Hero.* New York: Scholastic (2012).

Goldish, Meish. *Ground Zero Dogs (Dog Heroes).* New York: Bearport (2013).

Meyer, Karl. *Dog Heroes: A Story Poster Book.* North Adams, MA: Storey Publishing (2008).

Learn More Online

Visit these Web sites to learn more about brave dogs:

www.akc.org/akctherapydog/about.cfm

www.cnn.com/2013/12/09/us/dog-heroes

www.pdsa.org.uk/about-us/animal-bravery-awards/gold-medal-dogs

Index

About the Author

Meish Goldish has written more than 200 books for children. His book *Disabled Dogs* was a Junior Library Guild Selection in 2013. He lives in Brooklyn, New York.